~~INTRUSIVE~~ LINES.

Angelica Luzzi

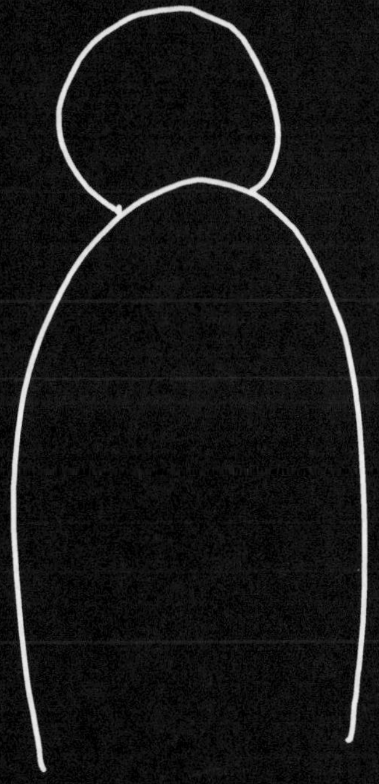

INTRUSIVE LINES.

(a collection of wanna be poems)

CASUALLY CRYING MYSELF TO SLEEP.

I kinda wish that I could write when I'm happy
to go back to these pages and smile between these lines
but during happy times my pen is dry

maybe I get my ink from the dark
writing in my parked car
nostalgia

I come back to this house made of paper only when it gets tough
roof made of my own thoughts
same thoughts that make it so tough

but when they collide in these designed lines
they sound bearable when they rhyme
they make a shelter for this grime

and all those words that would cut so deep
now like little soldiers in order
they come running to seal these wounds - ink like glue.

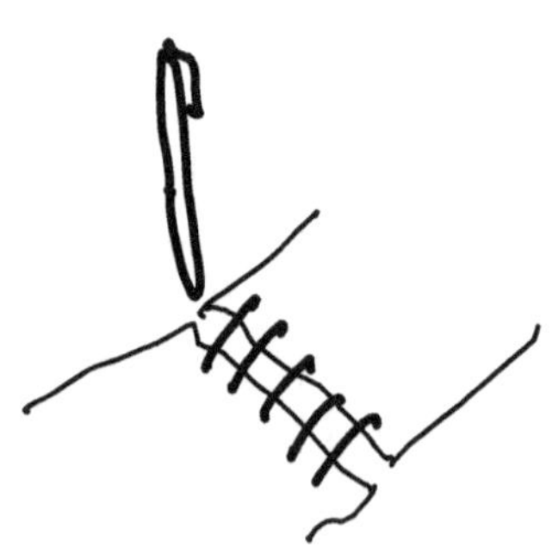

I'm so tired of designing you
or the one before you
or the one before that too

to match my colors with yours
I add shades I never wore

your angles too sharp for my soft skin
too loud or too quiet
you never match my pitch

never the perfect wave for me
I'm so tired of reinventing you
and lose myself in the sea

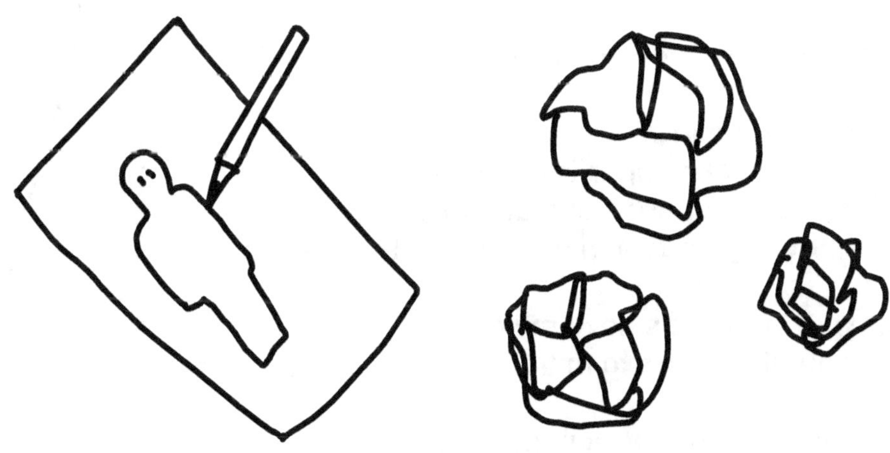

LET YOUR PROBLEMS HAVE MY NAME
SO I CAN GIVE YOURS TO MINE.

Let your anger kiss me
where I can hide it,
give my name to your lies
draw my face on your addiction
make the words of your father - mine

let your fear flow on me
but please, not on my eyes
I ran out of excuses after last time

Satisfy your craving
you know what's mine

You know I don't mind
We don't have to talk about last night
Trust me, everything is fine
You don't have to say that you are sorry
the fault was all mine

I won't call it the word they want me to say
We know it is the only way
We know it is not the same

I'll wear every face you want me to take

Why would I mind?
I like when your anger touches mine
I like when I cannot sleep at night
I like how my body aches between these lines

Let your problems have my name
so I can give yours to mine.

Just please, don't touch my eyes
I ran out of excuses after last time.

IN COMPANY,
BUT ALONE IN MY HEAD.

dejection,
sorrow,
disillusion,
rage

they die in my throat
like innocent soldiers
destined to a losing battle
destined to crumble
before they can reach the tip of my tongue

dejection,
sorrow,
disillusion,
rage

innocent soldiers
that will never see daylight
in front of you.

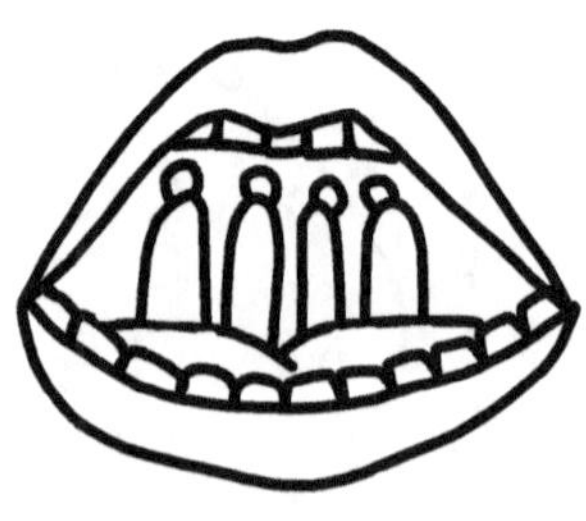

HONEY WORDS

I'm so tired
so exhausted
and hurt
so hurt
not any of your honey words
could heal this wound
so keep your lies to you
I need to be alone in my room
help this dust settle down
and then
when this dust becomes sediment
we can start this game again
but until then
im so exhausted
and hurt
so hurt
not even your honey words
could heal this wound.

and I wish I could say that I'm a writer
so that I could explain the disturbing amount of time
I spend every morning in my notes app

and I wish I could say that I'm a writer
so that I could forgive myself
for letting myself spiral every night
between these lines.

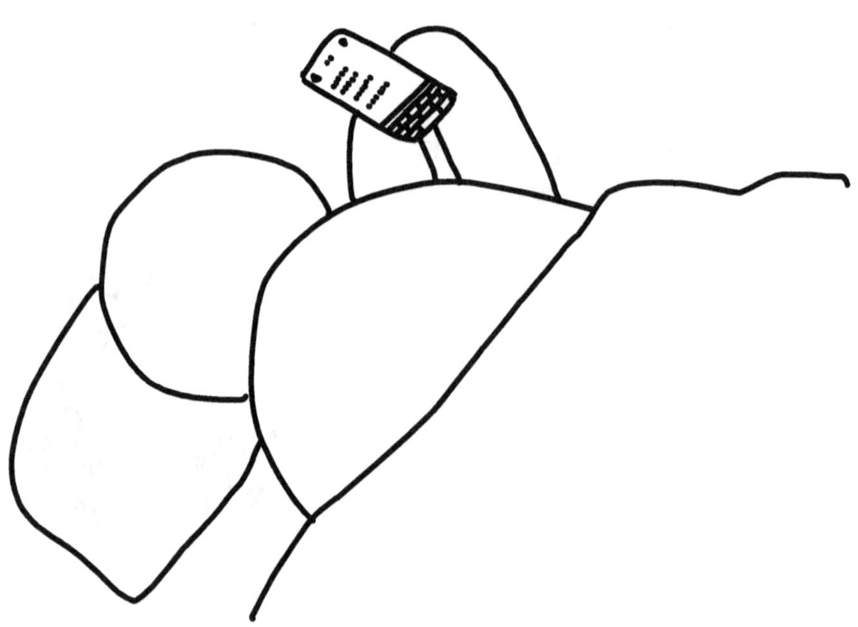

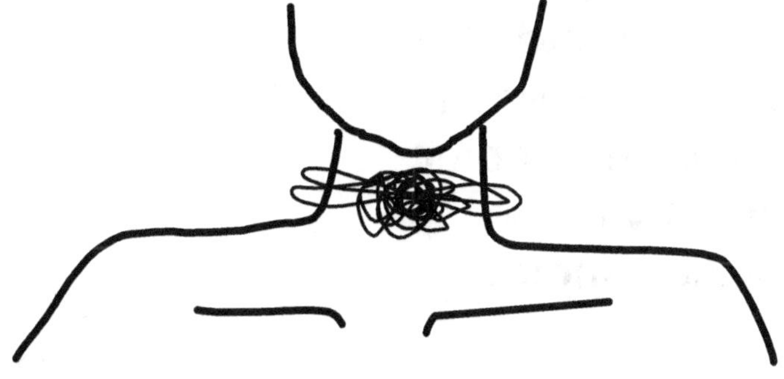

we are still undeniably and uncontrollably wrapped together like the knot that wraps my throat right now.

Picasso said he wished he had the mind of a kid,
to see what they can see
free from the constructs that growing up and
learning built unconsciously in our heads.
Or at least this is everything I remember from the
art history class I took.

And I, just like Picasso, wish
I could have the mind of a kid,
to fall asleep a little easier,
to wake up a little happier,
to stop biting my nails
to love you like I should.

14

I wish they knew you
so that they could see
why my colors are still stained from yours
years after you were gone

this is where I had to ask you to kiss me back,
but smiled when you left

trigger trigger
triggered me again
remember this taste of rejection
no worries! it's under the doormat
triggered this feeling as if he never left

blurring memories
blurring nights
blurring sight
tears
oh look who's back!

welcome sign
welcome back feeling that never left
welcome back
oh look who's back!
thanks,
now your face looks like someone else.

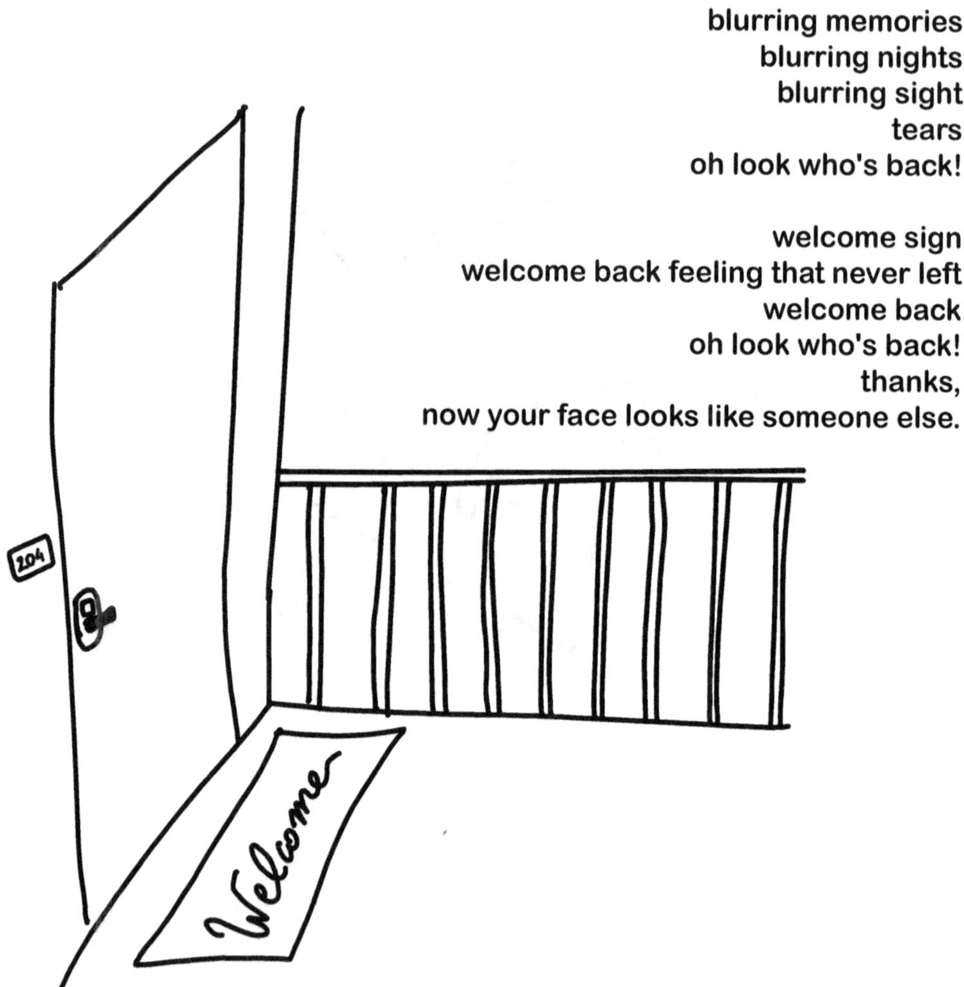

with you it felt like shoveling cement looking for water.

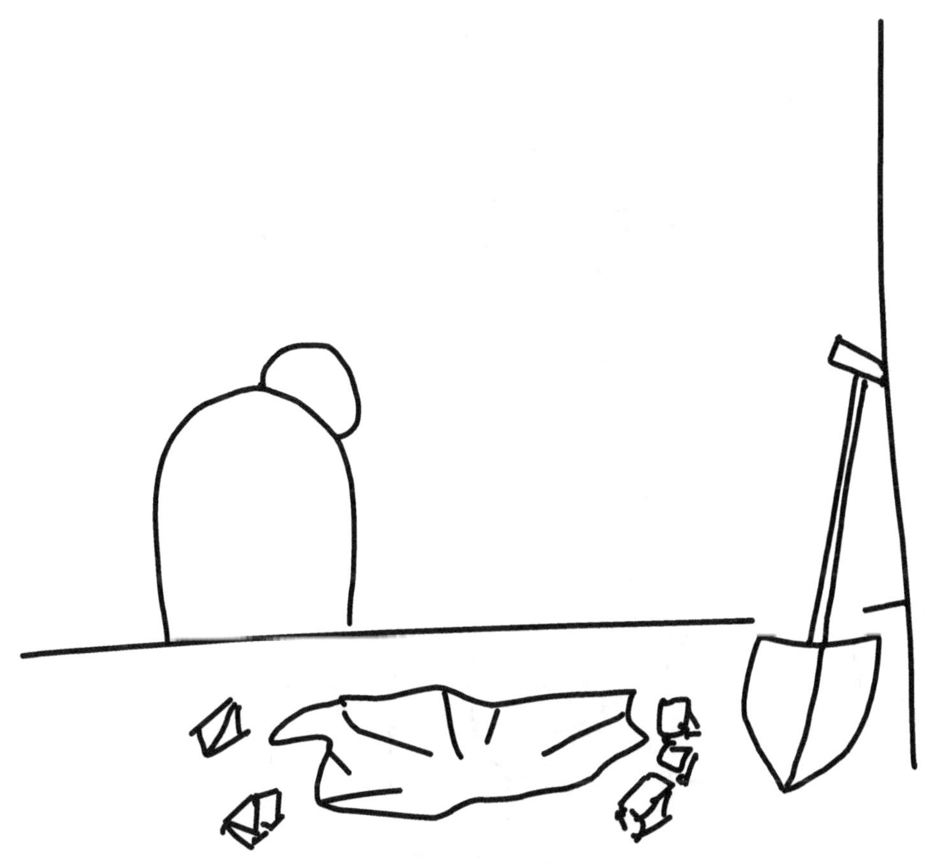

so sad that I can't be your first love
so sad you won't be mine
will we find a way to make this one worth the time?
or will it be only a bump during the drive?
pictures in your camera roll taking up space in your storage
will you delete them yourself or will you do it for her?
our stories, the ones you told your friends
will they be worth repeating them?
when the heart next to my name will disappear
and the room will get cold when someone mentions this year
will you gift our memory a tear?

In Italy we would say
"la lingua batte dove il dente duole"
which would traslate to
"the tongue reaches for where the tooth aches"
Maybe that explains why I keep reminiscing about it.
My tongue loves to linger around this pain.

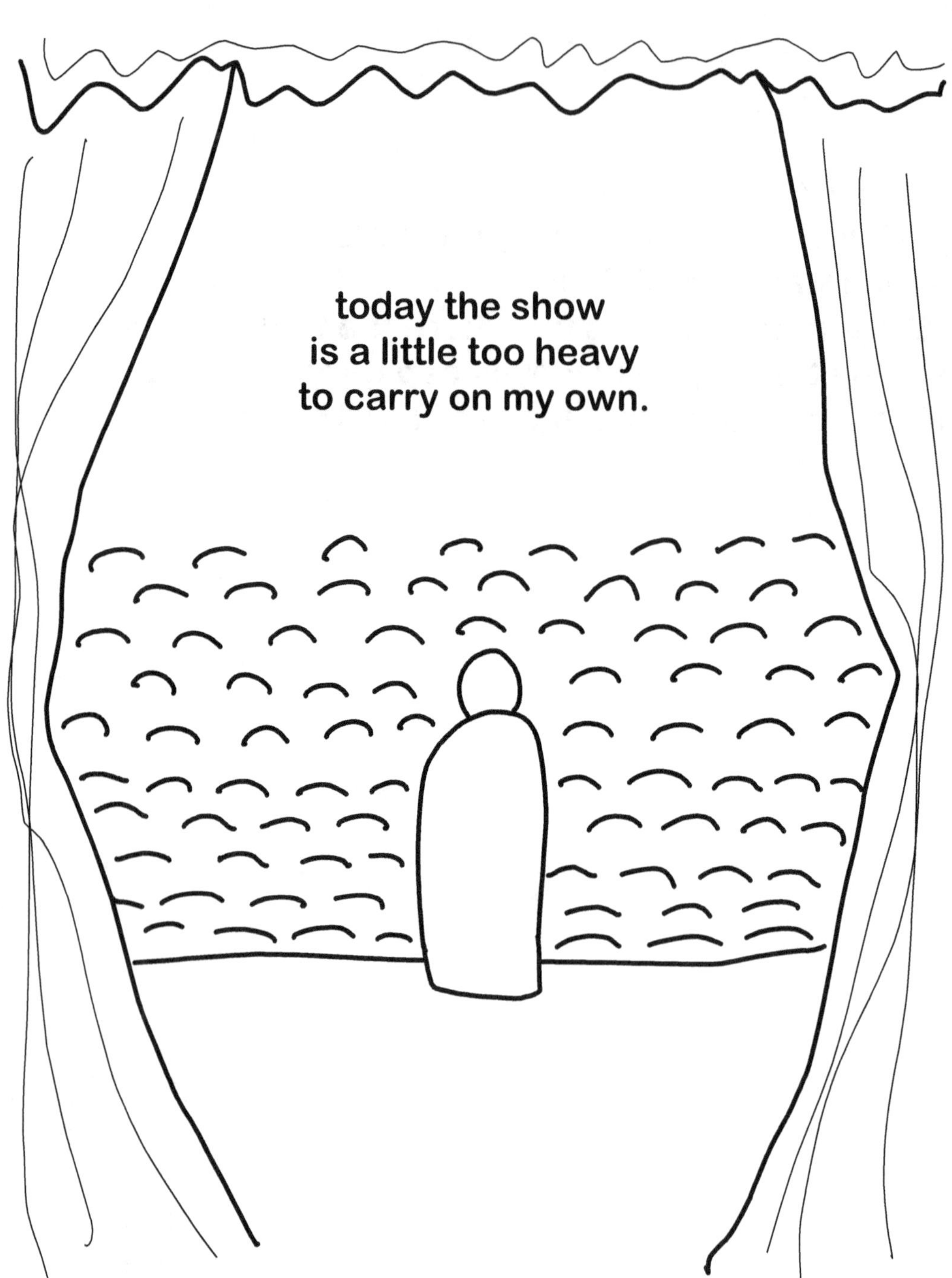

today the show
is a little too heavy
to carry on my own.

there is no image on the box
but I'm sure I'm missing pieces...

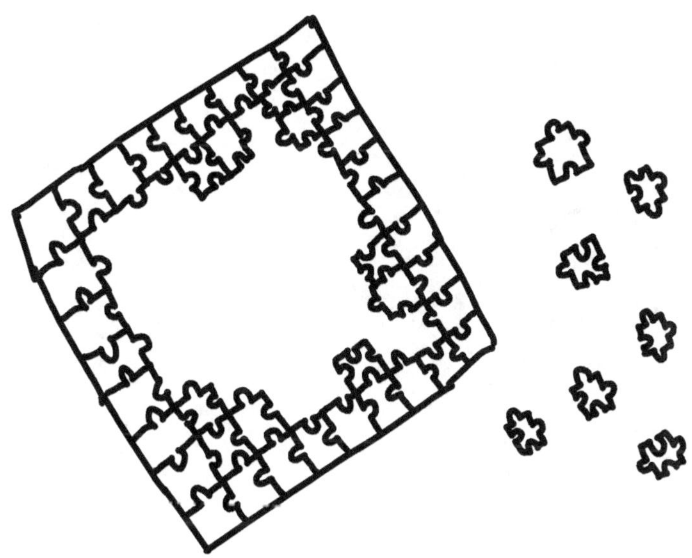

it's gonna be okay
at the end of the day
it's a beast I know by name.

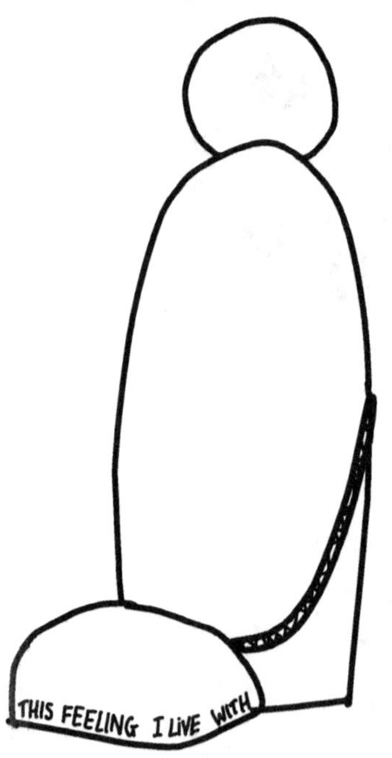

time to feed the demons!

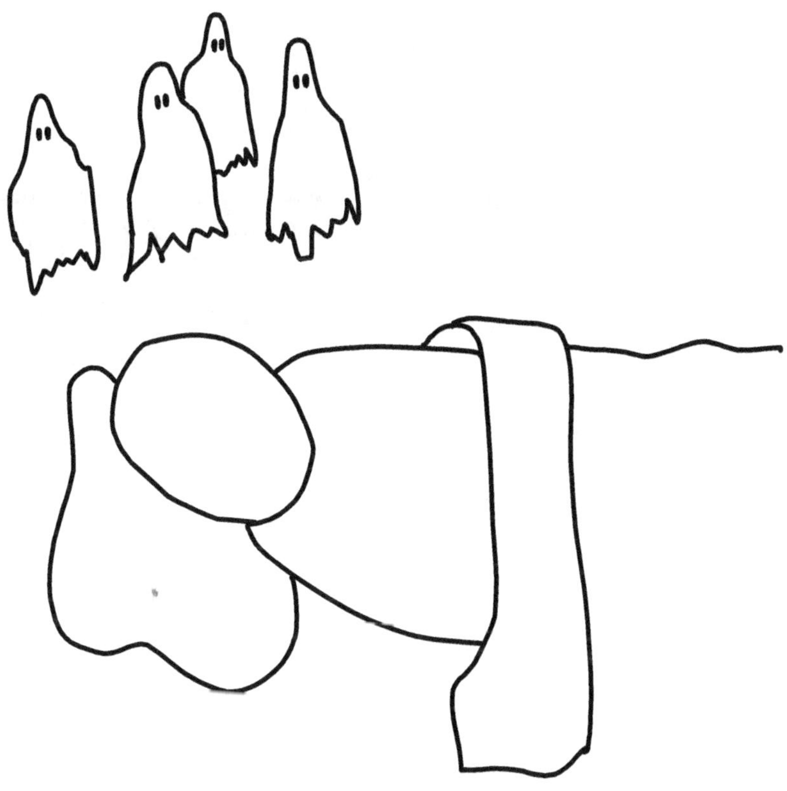

SELF-CARE.

BABY SOCKS

When I was a baby,
I loved to play the "Why?" game
driving my parents crazy
"Mommy why do we smile?
"Why do we sleep at night?"

But when I couldn't fit into baby socks anymore,
the questions got louder
I started playing a different game,
the "What's the point?" game
and you cannot win at this game
the issue is that
once it starts
it can get so dark
it's hard
to find an exit.

But then my sister's belly grew so much over the summer,
And now I have baby socks on my nightstand
smelling like baby powder

They gave her my name
Maybe you can win at this game
Maybe it's not too dark,
Maybe it's just too bright you cannot see.

let me see what life I can live today.

there are jumps
you won't be ready for

but the worst that can happen
is that you will have to try again

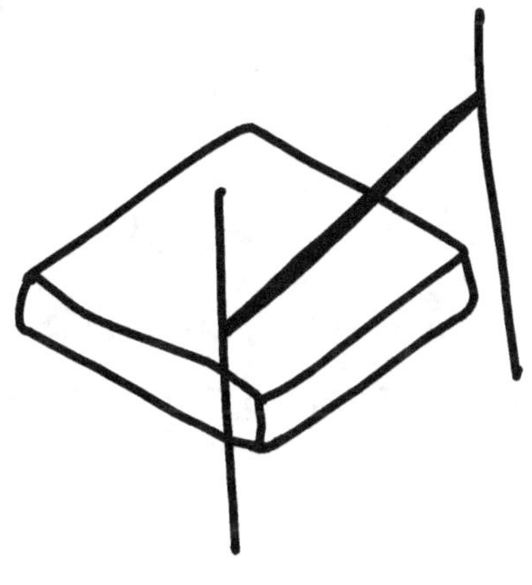

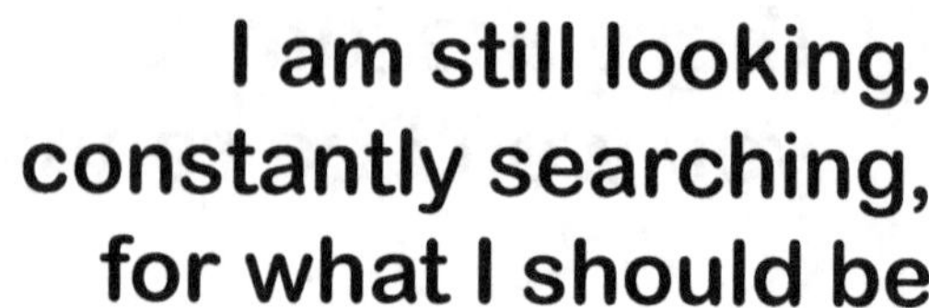

I am still looking,
constantly searching,
for what I should be

but all I see around
is who I've been
shades of me
the girl I used to be

I keep wondering,
looking for a grip

maybe this is it
maybe this is how
it is supposed to be

I'm gonna run after this feeling for the rest of my life.

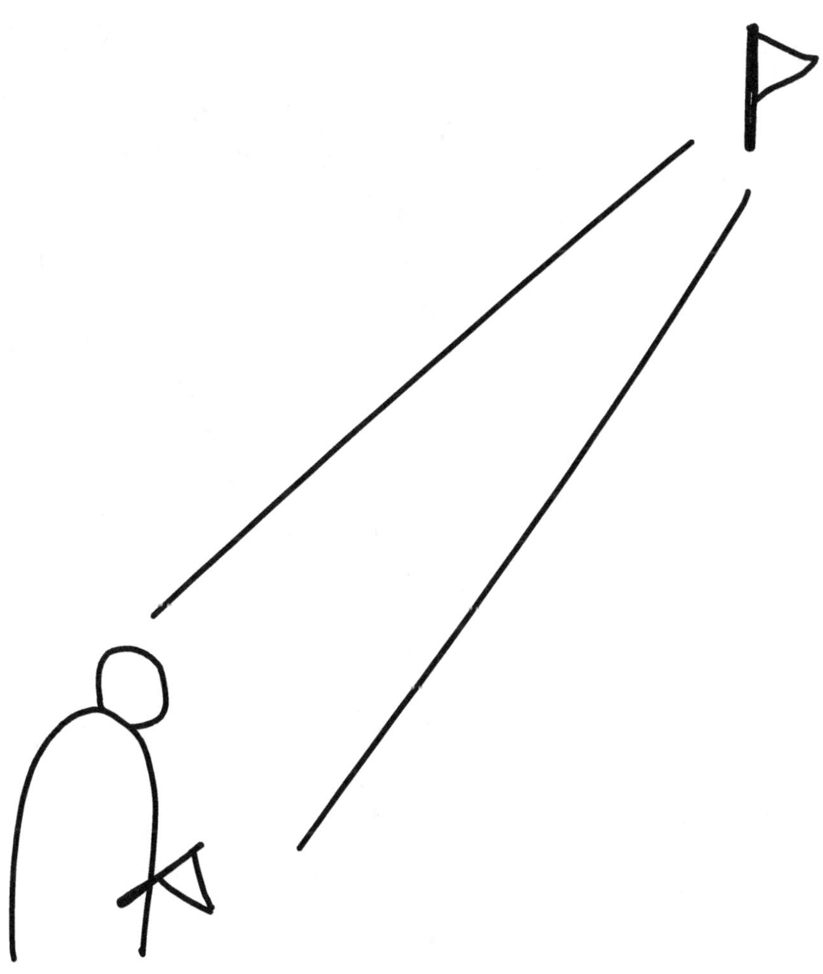

**Mamma says I can move mountains,
but mamma these look huge right now.**

sit down to this table
let's have this coffee talk
talk about your goals
while I watch the foam dissolve

wish I could listen to you
but how could I
when you keep starting sentences with only "I"s

you're so obsessed with yourself
but that's nothing new
I'm obsessed with myself too.

Don't make Nonna Maria sad,
go grab a snack!

you look beautiful honey.

little star
you've arrived so far
remember how loved you are

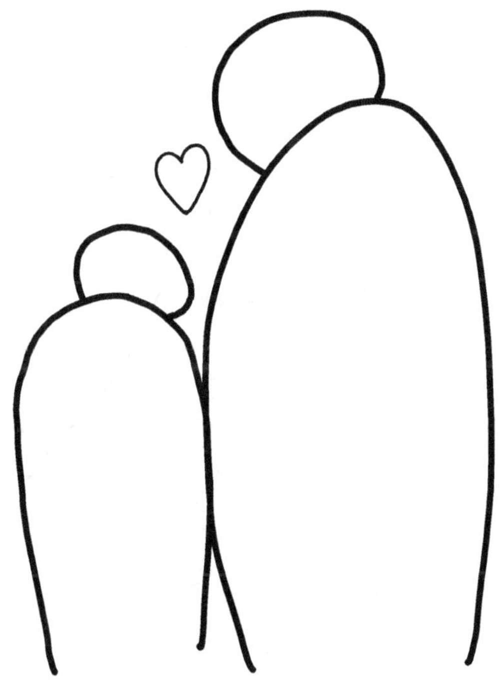

let your hands rest
you did your best
now get undressed
and go to bed
let your heart have some rest

all the words you said
all the tears you bled
now it's time to go to bed
get some rest
you did your best.

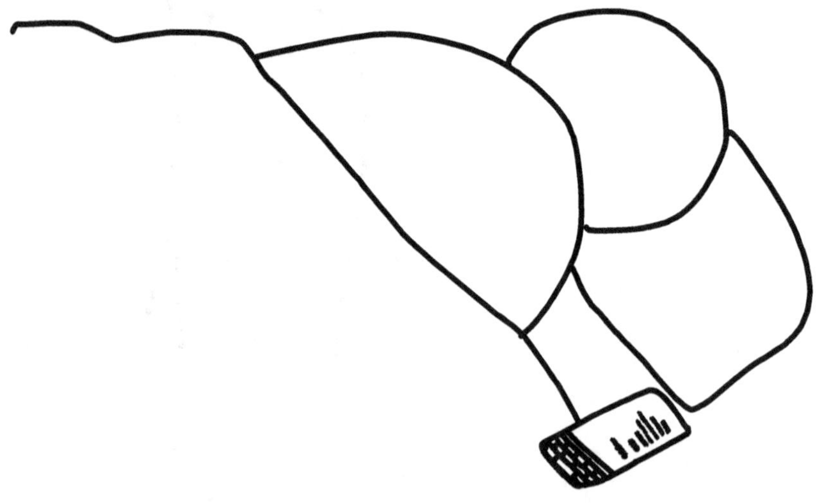

wearing black
but this is not a funeral.

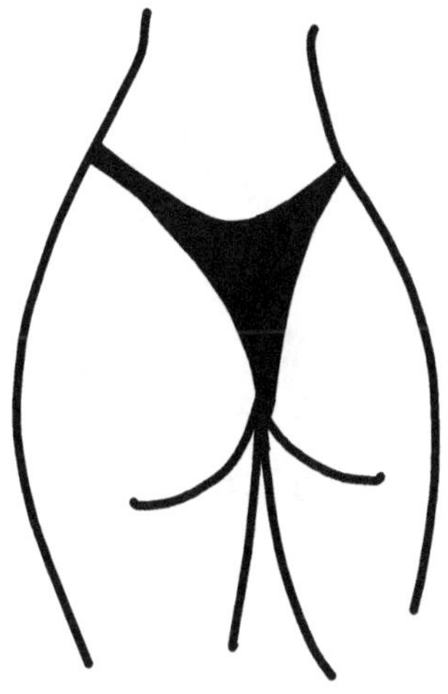

SIMP.

I wrote so many lines
about you

my hand hurts

but my ego hurts
the most

37

and if you don't like this one
I have plenty of more characters I can play
do you like her?
do you like it this way?

I have a portfolio you can choose from
I can stay in anonymous
tell me what you like best
I can morph into something just like that.

I would accept sharing you
let you be you
let you do your thing
I'll do mine

I would accept
seeing someone else's hand in yours
if I would still feel your warmth
if I would still feel desired

I would accept sharing you
if that meant having some of you
if that meant calling you mine

yours
if I can call you mine.

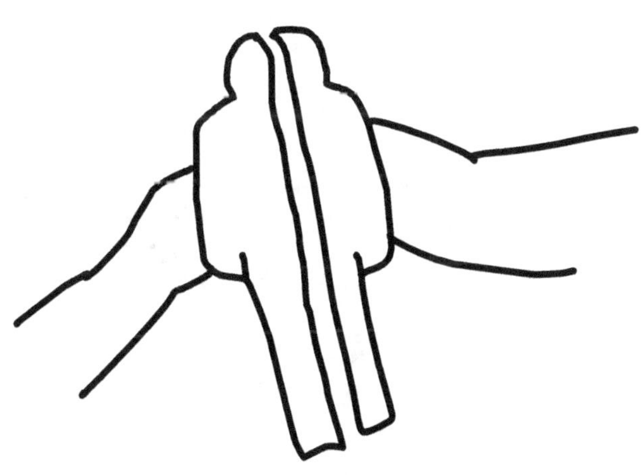

holes to breath
I keep the memory of you in a box,
too attached to let you go,
too hurt to keep you close.

oh baby,
we speak different languages
but you are the only one
that ever undertood me.

I write love letters in my head
telling you all the things I don't allow
myself to let you know.

I see a potential in you
that's even hidden from your own eyes
you tell me you don't look good
but why would I lie?

silk skin
you slide so good on me
how can you not see?
marble, sand, and wind
created by nature
a natural force

my ink source
I could write kilometers of lines
around your damn eyes
but we don't have time
It's time to go to sleep
11:11 baby make a wish

I wish you could see it too
I wish you could see yourself
from my point of view.

43

even the tears I cry are sweet in my mouth
when they taste like your name.

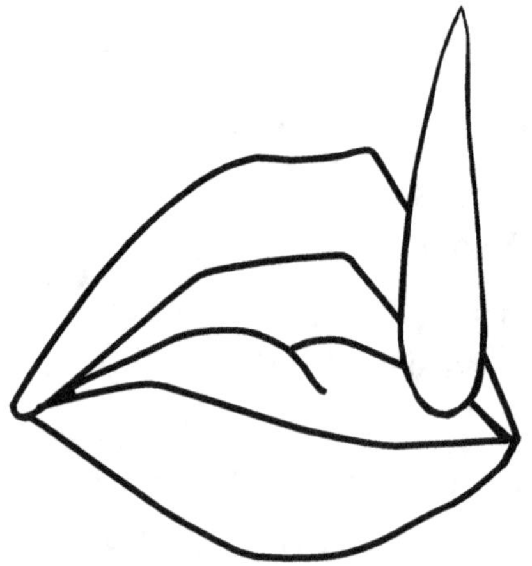

MINE TO KEEP.

I close my eyes
you are still driving my Jeep
I keep the memories of you close to me
even if you were never mine to keep.

You can tell how this feeling is deep
from how I kept loving you in secret
even when you were never mine to keep.

Every morning - and before going to sleep.
even though you will never be mine to keep.

But baby,
I won't let my thoughts leak,
because you are not mine to keep.

I know
I shouldn't be writing about you
but what can I do?
my pen loves to trace lines around you.

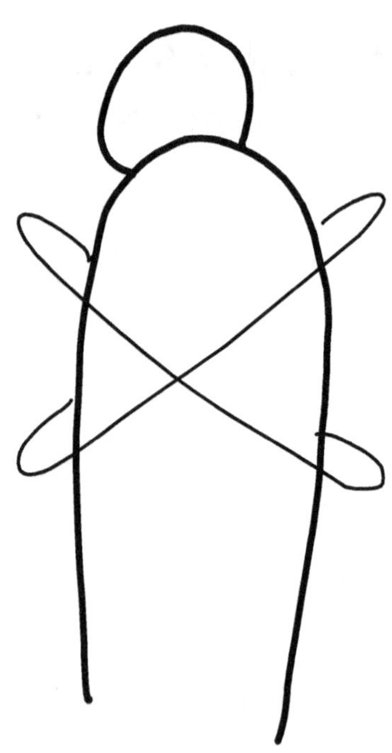

in here,
I can spend with you
as much time as I want.

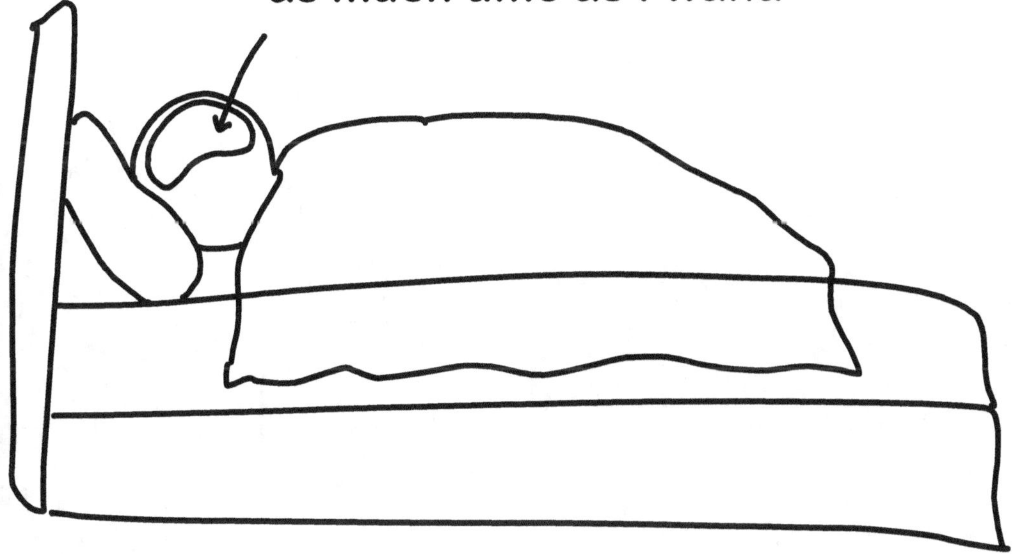

just like a toddler
begging her mother to pick her up
in her arms
here I am
begging you to hold me closer
does my love weigh too much?

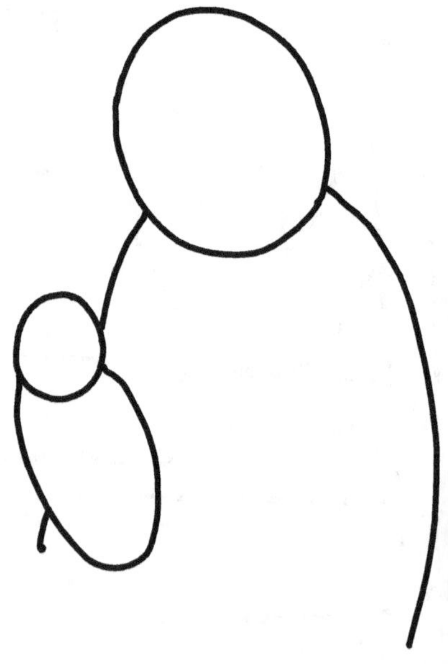

writing on my notes app
everything I want to tell you
because my ego's too big to surrender
but so is my love.

je ne regrette rien.

I'll be here on your shelf

waiting for you to get tired
of your other toys.

I miss you
even when we are
skin 2 skin.

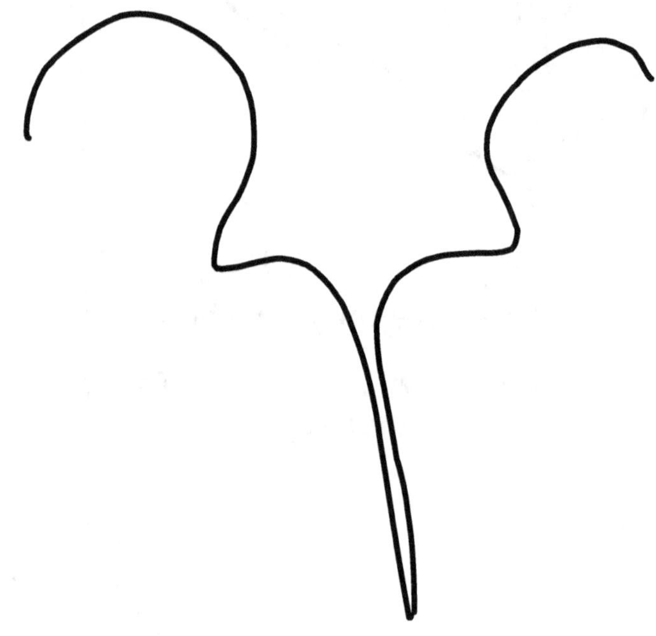

It was fall
when I fell for you
just like an innocent leaf
now my back is laying on the ground
and I'm staring at what I used to be.

STRAINED DOG.

Like a strained dog
I have to beware of your instability
your rotten anger
your trust issues

Yet,
I keep trying to pull you closer
covering my bleeding hands
wrapping my fingers in your lies
in order to pull you closer
trying to take care of you
but you care of nothing but yourself

I get it,
like a strained dog
you're hurt
but why would I even want you
when you won't even let me close?

strained dog
I'll watch you from afar
but my foot stays in the door.

OBSESSED.

I wish I could write
without you in my mind
but regardless how much I try
your face leaks between these lines
and fills every blank space
between the words I chose over your name.

Hate me one more time
make me bleed out one more cry

I dare you

drown my obsession in this lust
feed my disorders with memories from the past

don't give up
I dare you

let's make this agony last.

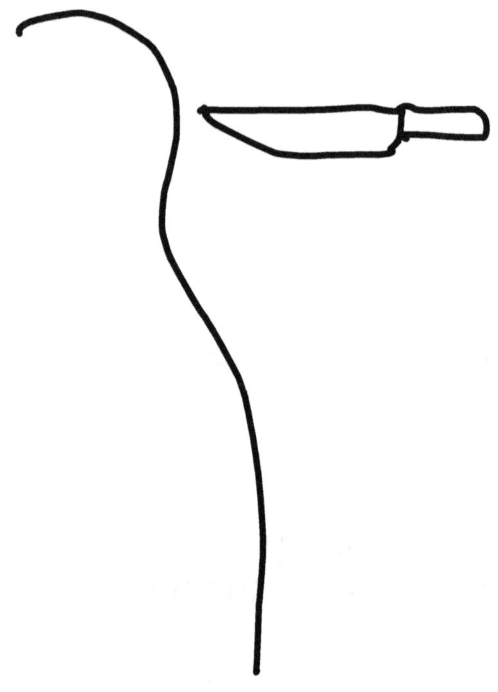

held hostage by my own thoughts.

the beat of your heart
matching mine
I can feel you panic
and so am I
silence
filthy lies
we shouldn't be doing this
if they ask, we are gonna deny
we know we will pay the price
for this expensive game - we're playing tonight
we should have thought this twice
but boring would be a poem about doing what's right.

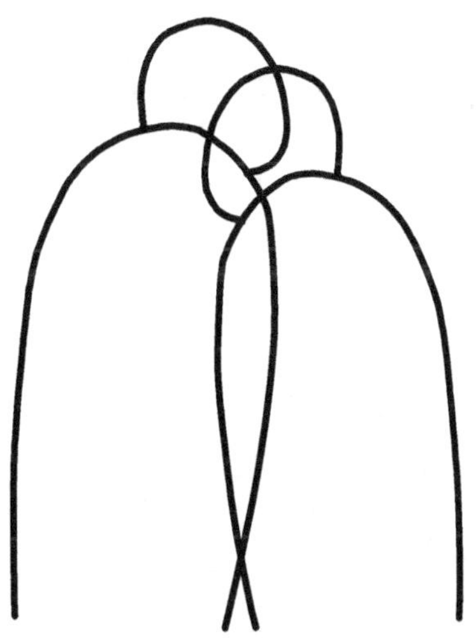

I take screenshots in my mind.

still alive
for that one drop of attention
you give me once in a while

for that one drop of attention
that I crave so bad
that keeps me wanting for more

for that one drop
that keeps me around.

and there is no shower,
where I don't think about you.

maybe I'm obsessed about losing you
because that's what I do
I fall so quickly - and you could too

we are as weak as a promise
a fear that is chronic
there's always space for someone new
if I could I would shut your eyes with glue
tell me that I'll always be the only one for you.

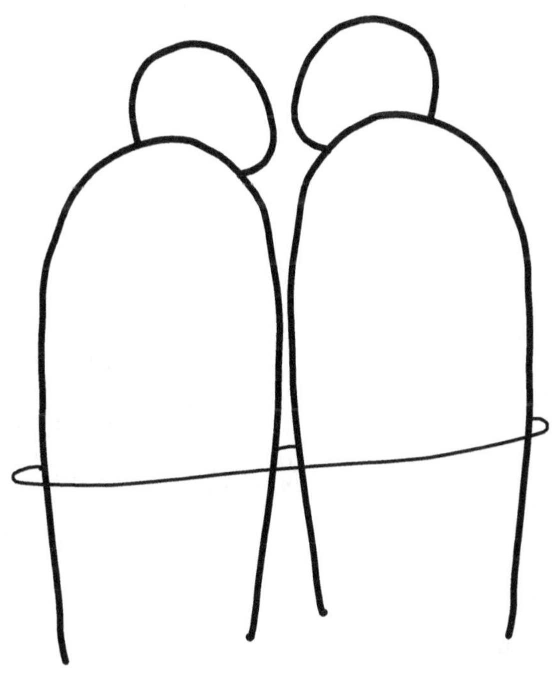

snap me back
I feel out of breath
all this craving
just to get a text
all this time
all this pressure
between the words I write
just send a sign
tell me one more lie
snap me back
so I can pretend you care.

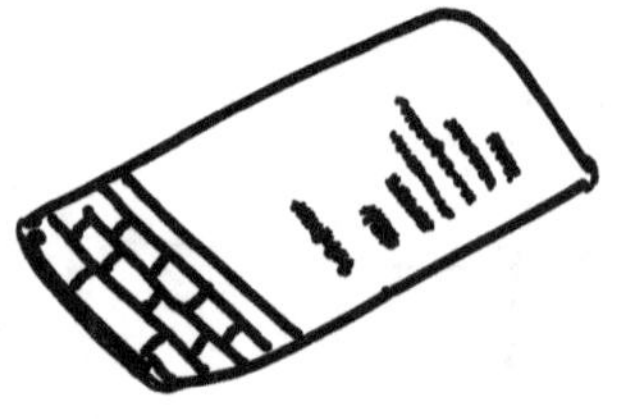

YOURS TO HATE.

slit my throat
cut me open
but then kiss the wound
I'm yours to hate.

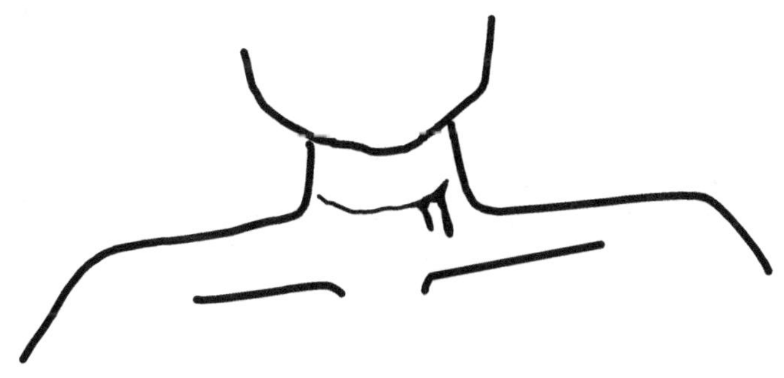

a new you is around the corner
a new face to put on a poster
under the word "wanted"
like a cowboy movie
I've been looking for you
but the face is always new.

SNAP MAPS.

I observe you from above,
look at you
living like my dogs in Nintendogs
your little figure on Snap maps
I watch you
listening to your little iPod and dance
or ride your cute little red car
away from me
I observe you from above,
like a Goddess
whose baby has been stolen from her.

lame lame lame
silly little words covering up your name
lame lame lame
silly little metaphors
I juggle around to explain your taste
lame lame lame
"I miss you" written on paper will be fed to flames
lame lame lame
silly me - silly hands - silly pen
I am the one to blame
blame this game I crave
to revive your taste
I pick silly little words from the trees
that grow on the path of your memories
silly me
I always end up picking the ones that sting
but hey,
lame lame lame
I am the only one to blame
you know I love this game.

never said the words I was dying to tell
I have been trying my best
not to let them slip out of my mouth
obsessed - they're all I can think about
forbidden letters - cuffed in my head
won't even allow myself to write them down
scared that they could be read
instead
I let them rhyme in my head
and then
rehearse before going to bed
the taste of them - all I can get out of them
I place them in order
let them slide down
from my head to my chest
yet, I never let out a sound
an ocean of secrets forced in a shell
boxed by fear
their box impossible to crack
never said a word
because I know you wouldn't say it back.

I know that life is a roller coaster,
I was remainded everytime you came but then you left
once blessed enough to have your head laying on my chest
the next minute we are back to back

seconds away from getting the trophy
seconds of glory
euphoria
then back to stalking your stories
back on my knees
please

I know that life is a roller coaster,
I was reminded everytime you came but then you left
and I know - it's not the best
but you know - I'm obsessed.

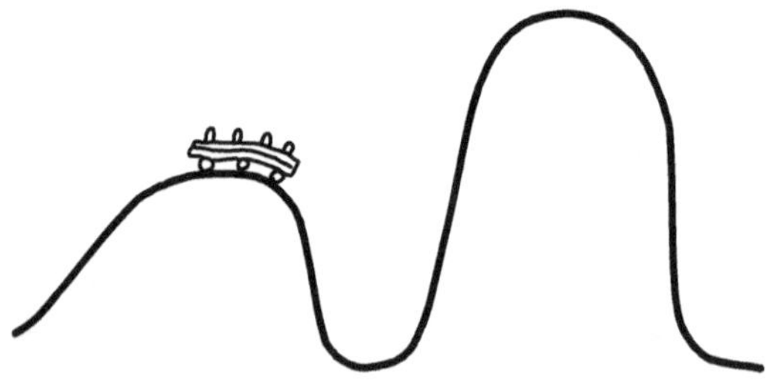

constantly out of breath
by running after you
so tired of chasing you
so tired of pretending to aim for you
when all I do it for
is to have something to pursue
we know what's the truth
I'm obsessed with this game
that happens to be dressed like you.

ALL MEN DO IS LIE.

My fear breaths in the beats of silence between your lies.

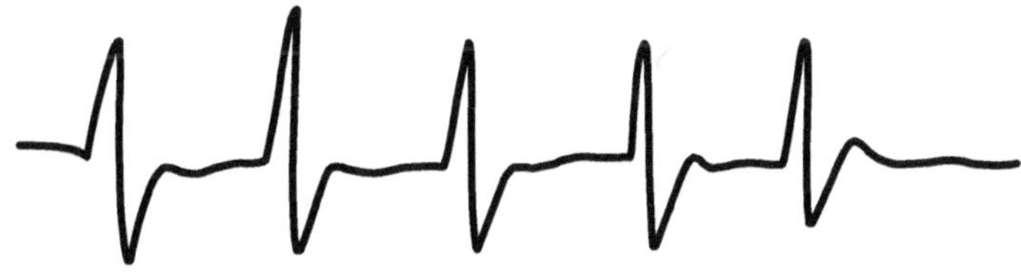

the sickness and the cure
a bruise
but the ice too
sea sick on this ship
but worth it for the view
I wonder for how long this will be fun
we are young
but I guess
this game won't be worth playing in a couple of years
so choose a lane
decide what to claim
behave
good boy
be good
or just a boy.

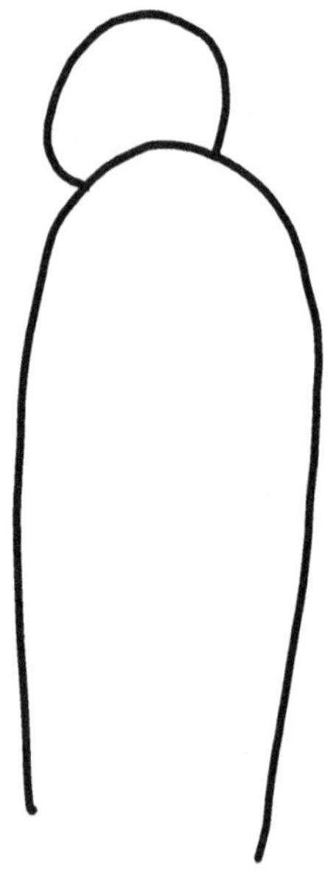

I thought your problem
was that you simply cannot commit

but it's easier than this

you only love others
when they treat you like shit.

so many red hearts in this chat
seems like your ego is bleeding.

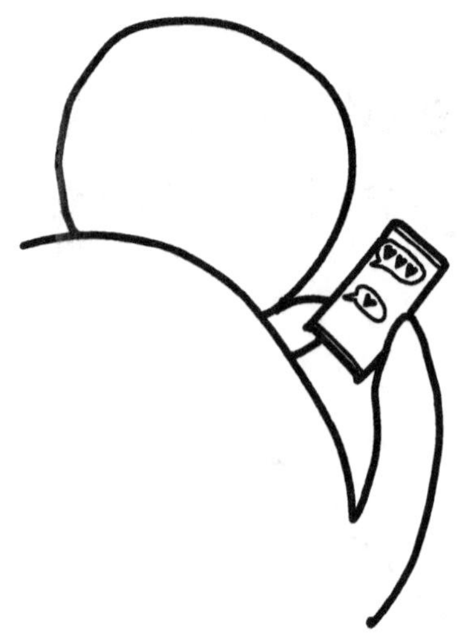

you played me like your piano,
but you know I love watching you play
you know I love this game.

how powerful to be grey
I wish I could
just like you do
mix your blacks and your whites like I cannot do

sometimes I go to sleep black
sometimes white will do
sometimes I even wake up blue
I'm so jealous of you

fuck, I really wish I could too
fade these feelings in something new
create a new shade of grey that is my own truth

but fuck you
honestly, how can you?
how can you stop those waves when they aim for you?
how can you not turn black under some charcoal rain?
how can you not turn pale when joy floods your brain?

fuck you
I wish I could do that too
enjoy this middle ground without falling for you.

THE GAME.

I started craving your attention
the day you denied it to me

I started sticking nails on my fingertips
abusing my hair with heat

anything for you to notice me

started crafting my words like a play
obsessed with this game
I boxed my personality away.

I don't even listen to you when you talk
not in the way you would want
like chess - your turn is my moment to think
what is my next move gonna be?

shaping my strategy below your rambling lies
yes baby, let's play one more time

83

I know nothing about you
but please
let's keep it this way
your character loses points
if it gets out of the shade

leave room for my expectations
there will always be time to burn that castle.

even if it's just for one night
let my fantasies borrow your face one last time.

never once it was about the boy
but always about the game.

APNEA.

there's a few things I want to remark
starting from the start:
I belonged to you since the beginning
when our hands met in the dark
every touch felt like winning
in a game I wasn't planning on partaking
I found my barriers thinning
under your occasional touch.

when intimacy felt like sinning
when I wasn't allowed to ask for much
I stood there waiting for you to see me
stood there hiding my feelings in plain sight
for you to look past

I was shouting my affection in that silence
but my words remained silent
I thought I was so loud, already
the ground under my certainties had never been more unsteady
I wanted to bite on the chains that kept me tied to that feeling
I tried to give myself time for healing

I would find myself upset
when you were about to leave,
your denial so loud
I felt like a fucking clown
my goal impossibile to achieve

5

I was studying for a class
I knew I would never be able to pass
my hopes hiding behind a wall of glass
showers would drag away in the drain
tears that had your name

then good moments would come
fresh like bare feet on grass
I never felt more dumb
"this time it might be the last"
"I wanna make this last"

I would threaten myself
it was my fault if I wasn't enough
fear of losing you embedded in lust
feelings always in contrast
even good moments felt like sunsets
awaiting a night of silence

mine for few seconds
before it felt like too much
and we would go back to the start

9

I know it's a game to lose
impossibile to win - a myth
but I never got to choose
even when
you were never mine to begin - with

10

I swear I was smart
before I opened my heart
but your name rhymes so sweet in my mouth
even when it hugs words of displeasure
you are all I wanna write about

even this pain feels like a treasure
constantly swimming in this doubt
when I'm around you, apnea.

still,
I have so many things to thank you for

it might have been a war
but one worth fighting for.

12

also, thank you for the pain
you know I'd do it all again

and thank you for the sparks of joy
so dense they couldn't be contained
think about those
when you get on that plane

this time, we might have lost a train
but the memories will stay
you cannot take them away
"maybe one day"
"maybe it will feel the same"

14.

when all we have is today
kiss me goodbye one last time
and when my lips won't be the last ones you kissed
and when my claim on you will wash down the drain
think about me when the sky is grey

you will be gone,
but this promise will remain,
"maybe one day."

besties.

you heard me read so many lines
about loves that were meant to
break

and you stood there listening
ready to wipe my tears away

you heard me read so many lines
of love stories that felt fake
meanwhile,
you were the realest of them all,
throughout all the way

loved me through all my mistakes
there for me when I would break
fuck - even the idea of losing you aches

for you I would do whatever it takes
going to our room at night to give you updates
impossibile to replace

filled my heart even when it would break
you where there through it all - with such a grace

so much fun - so much joy
but only so much because you where there
to share it with me
whether it was about a boy
whether it was about an interior designer degree

4

spitting lines at night
"I bet you won't"
"Bitch I might"
I can rant about lovers all I want
but you are the ones I'll think about on that plane
with you I even enjoyed the pain
same souls, different font
"Bitch you are gonna cry? STOP!"

I'm trying my best to explain
but random metaphors is all I got
I only write about boys - but maybe this time I forgot.

LONGER PIECES.

Sediment.

I have been living in cohabitation with this sorrow
the type of sadness that is so ancient
it lays as a sediment down to the level of my feet
rises if you dare to touch on it

dare to blow on that sand
and its dust will climb up
blur your sight
revealing tears you forgot to cry

you could never tell
standing there on your feet
so far away from me
the way that I feel
and all the memories I'll never reveal

you could never tell
standing there on your feet
a wall of glass between you and me
a mirror for some
who do you even see when you look at me?
is it me or is it what you see of yourself in me?

There are so many shades of me you still have to meet
But maybe it's better like this

You wouldn't like me if you saw me in daylight
I have scars that are impossible to hide

For now,
stay there in your doubt
there are truths you should live without.

Grandma's Old Mocha.

I never feel fulfilled in my perpetual run-up in preparation for that leap that perhaps will never happen - or that perhaps I am already taking - an unconscious arc in my daily normality.
Why do I always feel unspoken?
The feeling of unexpressed potential under the arch of my feet like the faint flame that heats grandma's old mocha; but in these five minutes the coffee does not arrive.
Yet I sit close - keep my eyes focused of the flame.
At 11, one remarked I spoke like a woman, I was told to behave like the little girls my age - but I didn't enjoy their games and I asked too many questions... perhaps uncomfortable for some.
At 22 the same alienation feeling remains.
I feel uncomfortable among adults and even more misfit among my peers.
I'm not comfortable with myself either - often overwhelmed by the feeling of being buried in an avatar that I cannot comprehend in terms of mechanics or physics as well as objectives.
I have those funny moments at night when I smell that long-awaited coffee, moments in which I try to project the plausibility, the intention, yet they never last long enough to show me the way, to show me the how.
Will grandma's mocha ever whistle?

Short Story:
"Yours to hate."

It was there, outside of my kitchen window, staring at me from the distance.

Undeniably mistreated, probably neglected, possibly abused.

It was there outside of my kitchen window, looking at me straight in the eyes as if we already knew each other. I got out of the house, crossed the road, and went straight to it.

My mom used to tell me to beware of stray dogs; they can bite you. You have to keep in mind that they are unstable.

I approached it, offered a hand to the level of its nose. I had never seen more striking eyes.

"Hey baby, are you okay? Are you lost?"

It immediately reached for me. Offered his head for me to pet, and I did.

I had never felt anything like that.

My hand belonged to him; my hand was his from the first moment we touched.

"Do you want to come home with me, baby?"

I don't even know why I asked; mine was his – from the first moment we touched.

What I had to offer was his to take, from the first moment we touched.

Blood rushing, sensitive skin, foggy brain – I couldn't see. And that is how it all begun.

I fell in love with him the first time I met him on the curbside outside of my kitchen window. I fell in love utterly, deeply, and irrevocably for a nameless dog whose temper was still unknown.
We would go on walks almost every day. We would spend days inside too. We would stare at each other's eyes for what seemed to be eternity. I couldn't even remember how my life looked before he got into the picture of it.
Lay next to me, let me take care of you.

My friends would pass by sometimes. They would stay for the trill of a drink or the ephemeral joy of a joint. They liked him.
Why wouldn't they? Maybe mom was wrong.

Sarah liked him particularly. She would bring him outside for a walk, without me, or fill up his bowl, without asking me. Me and Sarah had been friends since middle school, that was the number one reason why I don't see her anymore. Me and Sarah had been friends for over ten years, but she like him, particularly.

That nameless stray dog never managed to find a name for himself. He remained nameless week after week.

A single name, a single word, could have never embraced all that was about him. Never I could ever find him a label when he was everything and everything was his.

We would go on walks until my legs would start to ache, and after a few days with him had passed, our walks would last even after my legs would start to ache.

I was on a walk with him when my phone buzzed. An email. An alien sign of an outside reality I almost forgot about. My classmate reminding me about the story I had to submit.
After he got tired, we went back home. We laid on the couch as our ritual implied. I traced the line of his figure with a hand, while the other one opened my laptop. I hadn't written anything since months before. I started to type, but my hands being busy implied my hands being taken away from him. His nose pushed against my wrist to get my attention, but in the middle of a sentence you cannot really stop? Or can you? I couldn't, at the time.
While my fingers kept their presence on the keyboard, his teeth took the place of his nose on my wrist.

The day after, I didn't call my mother as I would always do, in the morning. I wasn't feeling like talking with anybody at all. I woke up with him by my side and no work done to submit.
The day after that, we went on a walk again. And after that, we got back home and took our place on the couch again, my hands went back to the keyboard only to encounter his disappointment. His teeth found their way to my skin once again. My displeasure would die in my throat before the words would even reach the tip of my tongue.
That was his only way to show how much he desired to be with me. Those eyes raging against mine were only raging because of those who mistreated him.

I am sorry. You shouldn't have had to go through that, love. I am sorry.

As time went by, I found a way to write without taking away any of me from any of him. Showers would take a couple of additional minutes, and so would the cooking, or the cleaning. I would sneak lines and quotes between the shield of duties and errands.

My words would flow much smoother after his presence saturated my mind. I reached a point where I would enjoy the product of his anger, the marks left after his touch, because those moments would eventually lead to kinder words and softer nights.

Less of my skin showing when around others
who wouldn't understand your loving me.

Eventually the roles switched.
I would find more comfort between the hug of pages and ink, than the one I would get from laying next to him. But that realization would remain untold.
Moments of murky mind would find their place on papers not to be read. I would whisper secrets between those lines, hide truths behind fictional faces that didn't look like mine.
My mom called one morning. I would have avoided the blurry eyes, the sour words she told me, the realization that she didn't say any lie. But there was no more time left to push back what had been kept hidden for too long.

Truth is sharper than teeth sometimes.

When she came over, he didn't like it as much as he used to.
Big words and loud questions filled the kitchen while my incoherent hands would keep petting the reason behind all that crying.
She told me that he didn't belong with me in the first place.
I told her that I might not have belonged with him, but that I unquestionably belonged to him.
She told me he had to leave; he had to go back to the street where he came from. I felt the tingling hands of panic slithering towards my throat. "It was not his fault! They made him this way!"

The silence between my cries kept the reality untold; I liked the way he made me feel. I liked the sorrow that was imbedded in his company.

Even the tears I cry are sweet in my mouth when they taste like your name.
Cut me open, then kiss the wound, I'm yours to hate.

The day I realized how much I craved those fractures in the glass of our picture, was also the day he was taken away from me.
It was also the day I realized how much of me I had forgotten.

My personality had been buried under his weight for a period of time that felt infinite and brisk at the same time.
It took me days to see the bigger picture. It took me weeks to see what they were trying to show to my blind eyes.

Yet, I still find the bite of lust and nostalgia have the best of me at night, sometimes.
The perfection of his eyelids when asleep.
The smell of the morning on his skin.
The vacillating first soft touch after his anger would have finally collapsed.
I would miss him in secret, declaring my love only if soft-spoken.

I had to beware of your instability,
your unpredictability,
your rage,
your trust issues,
yet, I kept trying to pull you closer,
wrapping my bleeding hands in your lies.

I grew over the summer. I realized how my colors weren't faded, only covered in dust. I managed to manage the traces left from you.
I saw you one night, outside of my kitchen window, on the same spot where our eyes first met.

Undeniably mistreated, probably neglected, possibly abused.

I saw my reflection on the glass of the window in front of me.

Undeniably mistreated, probably neglected, possibly abused. But not anymore.

I stepped outside for a second only to place a bowl of water on the ground. Your eyes met mine. We both didn't make a sound.

I am sorry. You shouldn't have had to go through that, love. I am sorry.
But nor did I.

if you have arrived this far...
Thank you.

First of all, thank you to my family for always allowing me to follow my passion and for holding my hand on the way. Thank you to the San Diego squad (every-single-one of you) for being my support-system on the other side of the world, for giving me stories to write about, and for teaching me what family can look like. Words cannot decribe how much I love you guys. 204-ever.
Thank you to my besties from "il Book Club" - only you know how much you mean to me.
Thank you to all the friends I kept sending drafts to, or worse, kept reading out loud to - your courage and patience is highly appreciated.
Thank you to all the depressive episodes that gave me something to write about. As Laura once told me, "what's bad for the heart, is good for the art." (this quote is actually from Jandy Nelson, but let's pretend it's Laura's).
Lastly, thank you to all the boys I've been obsessed with
- it might be cruel that you've always been the fuel -
but if something works, why fix it?

until next time,
yours,
Angelica.